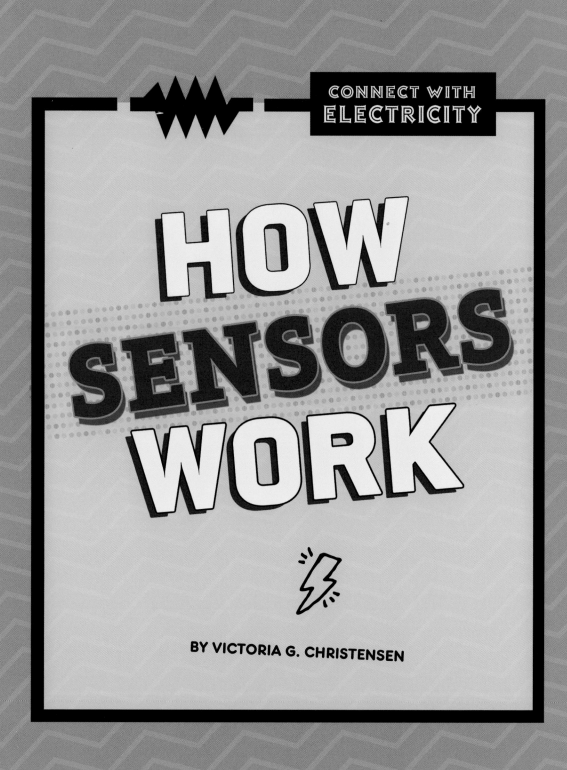

CONNECT WITH ELECTRICITY

HOW SENSORS WORK

BY VICTORIA G. CHRISTENSEN

LERNER PUBLICATIONS ◆ MINNEAPOLIS

Dedicated to my writing group:
Betty, Linda, June, Kristy, and Amy
—V.C.

Special thanks to content consultant Neal Clements, Adjunct Professor of Electrical and Computer Engineering, North Dakota State University

Lerner Publications Company
A division of Lerner Publishing Group, Inc.
241 First Avenue North
Minneapolis, MN USA 55401

For reading levels and more information, look up this title at www.lernerbooks.com.

Main body text set in Aptifer Slab LT Pro 12/18.
Typeface provided by Linotype AG.

Library of Congress Cataloging-in-Publication Data

Names: Christensen, Victoria G., author.
Title: How sensors work / by Victoria G. Christensen.
Description: Minneapolis : Lerner Publications, [2017] | Series: Connect with
    electricity | Audience: Ages 8–11. | Audience: Grades 4 to 6. | Includes
    bibliographical references and index.
Identifiers: LCCN 2015046092 (print) | LCCN 2015048958 (ebook) |
    ISBN 9781512407792 (lb : alk. paper) | ISBN 9781512410105 (eb pdf)
Subjects: LCSH: Detectors—Juvenile literature. | Physical instruments—
    Juvenile literature. | Sensor networks—Juvenile literature.
Classification: LCC TK7872.D48 C554 2017 (print) | LCC TK7872.D48 (ebook) |
    DDC 621.3815/36—dc23

LC record available at http://lccn.loc.gov/2015046092

Manufactured in the United States of America
1-39351-21163-3/1/2016

CONTENTS

Researchers can place sensors inside a football player's helmet or other gear to measure the strength of the hits he takes during a game.

INTRODUCTION

You walk into a store with your parents. Like magic, the doors open before you reach them. You go to the back of the store to use the restroom. The lights brighten on their own. When you join your parents at the checkout lane, the clerk is passing items by a scanner. It records the items and their price. Your parents pay for the groceries with a credit card. The credit card scanner reads the information on the card, and the transaction is approved.

All these events work because of sensors. These devices usually function behind the scenes in electronics we use every day, so we often don't even know when they are there. But sensors are important for more than just garage door openers or automatic toilets. Sensors can monitor a medical patient's brain or heart activity, detect a hard hit to a football player, and even keep track of astronauts' exposure to radiation during spaceflights. Sensors detect and respond to input from the environment. The input may be light, heat, motion, or other things that can be measured. Sensors can help us monitor the environment, keep us safe, and make life a little easier.

CHAPTER ONE

HUMAN **SENSORS**

Scientists and engineers study human senses in order to design better electronic sensors. Humans have five main senses. They help us see, feel, hear, smell, and taste. The brain and spinal cord make up the central nervous system and control the five senses. The brain interprets the information we receive through our senses and then sends messages to other parts of the body. The messages tell the body parts what to do.

Let's say you see a friend smiling at you. The following sequence describes what happens when you see your friend and smile in return: The light bouncing off your friend is called the *stimulus*. Your eyes are the *sensors*, taking in the light and helping you see your friend. They send that data to your nervous system, known as the *coordinator*. Your brain decides how to react and sends a message to smile to your face muscles. Your face muscles are *effectors*, or the parts that cause

Different sections of the human brain respond to different stimuli.

or perform a *response*. In this case, the response is to smile back.

Sensors detect signals. A signal can be a sound, a motion, or some other form of information. The sensor takes this information and responds to it. Sensors do this by changing one form of energy to another.

Scientists and engineers have tried to mimic human senses in robots. A robot gathers data about its environment. It uses that data to make decisions. Artificial sensors provide data to the robot. The sensors are controlled by a computer that acts like the human brain and commands the robot to act. The command could be to pick up an object or sweep the floor. Some robots can even smile.

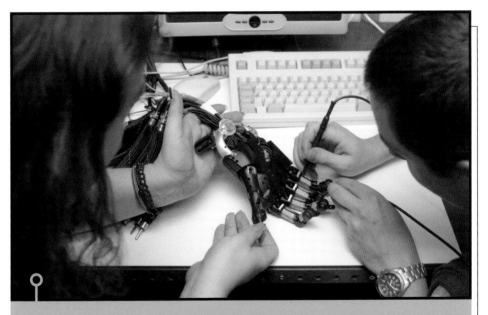

The sensors in some robotic body parts are so advanced that they can be used to replace the sense of touch a person may have lost!

Imagine a robotic vacuum. It can sense objects in its path so that it knows to change its route. The stimulus might be the wall. The vacuum has a bumper with touch sensors. When the vacuum bumps into the wall with its bumper, wires from the touch sensors send a message to the vacuum's computer. The computer is the robot's coordinator. It decides the robot should turn away from the wall, so it sends a message back to the motor, or the effector. The vacuum turning is the response.

This robotic vacuum's sensors will respond when it bumps into this coffee table.

THE RISE OF THE ROBOTS

Some science fiction books and movies feature robots that become smarter than their creators and want to conquer human civilization. Not all robots are as friendly as the hero in the movie *WALL·E*. But the real threat of artificial helpers may have nothing to do with evil robots. Humans might get too comfortable with robots making life easy. Some scientists are teaching robots how to make people laugh. A robot might tell you jokes while cleaning your room at the same time. Getting lazy might become pretty tempting!

Scientists who design and work with sensors know that human senses are good starting points to base their devices on. Just like our noses interpret different signals than our eyes, different types of artificial sensors are created to detect various signals.

CHAPTER TWO

THE SCIENCE OF SOUND

Sound is the vibration of air particles. We call these vibrations sound waves. Scientists use the term *oscillation* to describe the way sound waves move. Oscillation is a back and forth movement, like an oscillating fan.

WAVELENGTH AND AMPLITUDE

The words *wavelength* and *amplitude* describe the size and length of waves. They can describe sound waves or other types of waves, such as light waves or the waves in a lake or ocean. Some sensors work by detecting sound or light waves.

To understand wavelength and amplitude, you need to understand a little more about waves. A wave is a change that travels through a substance, sometimes called a medium. When sound waves travel through the air, the air is the medium. When ocean waves travel through the water, the water is the medium.

Amplitude is the height of a wave. It's measured from the crest, or top of the wave, to the midpoint of the wave. It can also be

DIAGRAM OF A WAVE

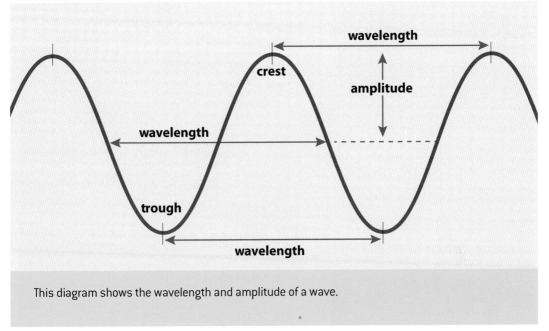

This diagram shows the wavelength and amplitude of a wave.

measured from the midpoint to the trough, or bottom of the wave. A really big wave will have a large amplitude, and a small wave will have a small amplitude. Some sensors detect amplitude. For example, scientists can use sensors to detect the strength of an earthquake. These sensors detect the amplitude of waves in a DVD player to detect its remote control.

Wavelength is just what it sounds like—the length of a wave. It is measured from the crest of one wave to the crest of the next. The crest is the top of the wave. If you think back to ocean waves, the wavelength is measured from the top of one wave to the top of the next. Some sensors detect wavelength, such as the one used in the remote control for a DVD player.

The coils in a Slinky move back and forth just like the medium in a longitudinal wave.

Sensors inside of microphones sense longitudinal sound waves. A longitudinal wave occurs when the medium moves in the same direction that the wave moves. Think of a Slinky as an example of a medium. You can hold a Slinky in your hands and push the end of the Slinky in your left hand toward your right hand. You'll see the coils move like a wave. They bunch together and move toward your right hand. Then the coils change direction and move back toward your left hand. This movement from one hand to the other is the wave. Sound waves are examples of longitudinal waves. Sound waves can bounce off an object like a wall and move in the opposite direction, just like the coils in a Slinky. We hear this bouncing sound wave as an echo.

FREQUENCY

Sound sensors can also detect the frequency of waves. Frequency is the number of times something happens in a given period. For example, if you take swimming lessons on Tuesdays and Thursdays, the frequency of your swimming lessons is twice a

BAT DETECTORS

Bats can determine distance with sound. They send out a sound, and an echo returns. The time it takes for the echo to return gives the bat an idea of the distance. Bats can also learn an object's size in this way. This bat sense is called echolocation. Scientists study these bat sounds. They use a bat detector with a sound sensor to study the echo and identify the bat species.

week. In waves, the frequency is the number of wave crests that occur in a certain time period. One complete rotation of a wave is called a cycle. Frequency describes how fast the crests go by, or how fast a wave is oscillating. Engineers measure frequency in hertz, or the number of cycles per second.

A microphone can pick up the low frequency of an acoustic double bass.

Sound travels with different frequencies. This creates different noises. A sound wave oscillating quickly will have a higher pitch, while a sound wave oscillating slowly will have a lower pitch. On a violin, a string will vibrate quickly and make a high sound. On an acoustic double bass, a thick string will vibrate slowly and make a low sound. These two instruments make different sounds, and therefore have different sound frequencies, because of the different lengths and weights of the strings. Some sensors, like a microphone, are designed to detect these sound frequencies.

To help understand how a microphone works, it's useful to know how humans hear. Humans hear when sound waves enter the ear. The sound is the stimulus, and the ear is a sensor. The sound waves cause the eardrum to vibrate, and that vibration is carried to the parts of the ear that are connected to nerve cells. These nerve cells send signals similar to electric currents. The currents travel from the nerve cells to the brain, which identifies

DIAGRAM OF A MICROPHONE

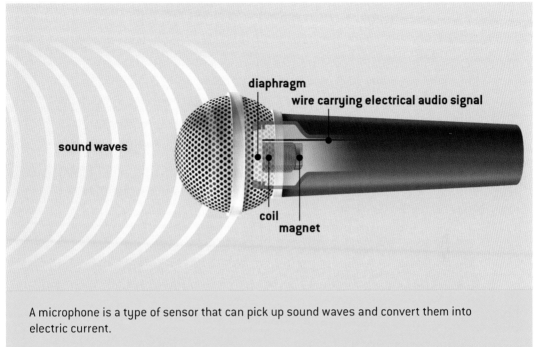

diaphragm

wire carrying electrical audio signal

sound waves

coil

magnet

A microphone is a type of sensor that can pick up sound waves and convert them into electric current.

the sound. Is that the smoke alarm or the alarm clock? The brain decides what to do based on the signals it receives. Your brain combines all the sounds you hear and helps you interpret them, so you can make sense of voices or other sounds such as music.

A microphone is a sensor that converts sound to electricity. This sensor works in a similar way to how our ears sense sound. A microphone has a diaphragm, a thin piece of material made from paper, plastic, or metal. When sound waves strike the diaphragm, it vibrates, which causes other parts of the microphone to vibrate. These parts will vibrate faster for sounds with higher frequencies.

SONAR DETECTS SHIPS AND SHIPWRECKS

Sonar stands for sound navigation and ranging. Sonar detects sound waves that travel through water instead of air. Scientists use sonar to help map oceans. They can map the seafloor and find underwater hazards or even locate ships and shipwrecks. There are two types of sonar. Passive sonar can detect noise from ships. Military vessels use it to "listen" to the ocean. Active sonar sends out a sound signal into the water. If the sound bounces off a shipwreck, for example, it returns as an echo. The time it takes for the echo to return tells the scientists the distance to the shipwreck.

One of the parts that vibrates is a metal coil. It moves back and forth in a magnetic field and creates an electric current. The electric current travels along wires inside the microphone to a speaker.

Microphones are used as sound sensors in many devices. Baby monitors and most laptops have microphones. Smartphones have microphones to receive sound commands and make calls. Many smartphones can receive your voice and convert it to text. Your voice is the stimulus that is detected by the microphone inside the phone, which acts as the sensor. All the information from your voice (wavelength, amplitude, and frequency) converts to an electronic signal. The computer in the phone receives this signal and turns it into text. The computer sends a message to your display screen (the effector) to show the text message (the response).

Some robots have sound sensors too. In a robot, a sound sensor senses the changes in air pressure from sound waves. Then it sends an electrical signal to the robot's computer. This is similar to the way ears send messages to the brain. The signal tells the robot's computer what to do, but the computer can only follow instructions that it is programmed to follow.

CHAPTER THREE

THE SCIENCE OF SIGHT

ur eyes are light sensors. They take in light from our environment. First, light enters the cornea, the outer layer of the eyeball. The light is refracted, or bent, by the cornea. The light is bent to direct it to the pupil, a small hole that is surrounded by the colored part of the eye. That colored part is called the iris. The iris changes the pupil's size to let more or less light enter. Light that enters the pupil goes through the lens, which allows the light to shine on nerve cells that are in the back of the eye. The nerve cells send signals to the brain. The brain combines these signals to make an image of the object you're looking at.

Some robots and devices such as cameras use optical sensors. *Optical* refers to vision, or sight. Like your eyes, optical sensors work by detecting light waves. They can measure the change in the strength of the light, or they can measure the interruption of light. Engineers have designed optical sensors that can detect visible, infrared, and ultraviolet light. Visible light is the only light that human eyes can see. Sensors on satellites detect visible light, observing

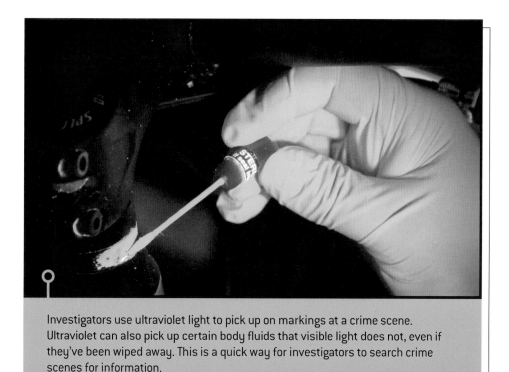

Investigators use ultraviolet light to pick up on markings at a crime scene. Ultraviolet can also pick up certain body fluids that visible light does not, even if they've been wiped away. This is a quick way for investigators to search crime scenes for information.

clouds and weather patterns on Earth. A TV remote sends pulses of infrared light, instructing the TV to change the channel or pull up other menu options. Police detectives use ultraviolet sensors to determine if an area at a crime scene contains blood.

Just as wavelength and frequency are important to understanding sound, they are also important to understanding light. Light moves even faster than sound because light has shorter wavelengths. With shorter wavelengths, there is less time between crests and therefore higher frequencies. Different light waves have different frequencies. Infrared light has a lower frequency range followed by visible light

FREQUENCIES OF LIGHT

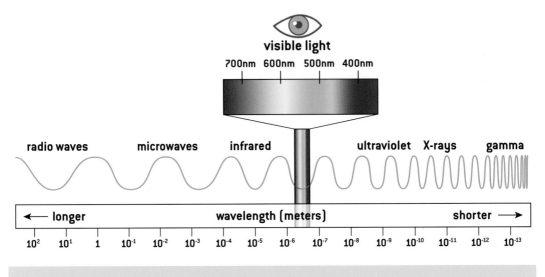

Different types of light have different wavelengths. Some types of light have very long wavelengths, and some others have very short wavelengths. Visible light is in the middle of the range.

and then ultraviolet light. Sensors can be designed to interpret the different frequencies.

Light waves are transverse waves. In a transverse wave, the medium doesn't move with the wave. Think of a football stadium where the fans do "the wave." The people in each section stand and put their arms in the air. Then the people in the next section follow by doing the same thing. This is how the wave travels through the stadium. The people are the medium, and their up-and-down motion is the transverse wave. They move up and down but do not travel around the stadium with the wave.

SOLVE IT!

THE POWER OF LIGHTS

You know that your TV uses a light sensor to receive signals from its remote. You push the Power button on the remote, and your TV turns on. But earlier when you walked into the TV room and flicked on the lights, the TV didn't turn on. Why doesn't your TV receive signals from the other lights in the room? *(The answer key is on page 35.)*

Optical sensors can also measure the interruption of light. This type of sensor is used for garage doors. It makes sure that nothing is in the way before the door closes. Optical sensors are also used for automatic doors at stores. When you step in range, you block the light. The sensor registers this, and the door opens.

To give you a better idea of how optical sensors work, let's look at the way we monitor water pollution with sensors. Most optical sensors both send and receive light signals. Water pollution sensors send out a beam of light that shines through the water. The light is reduced when it flows through polluted water toward a detector. Imagine shining a flashlight through a thin blanket. The light from the flashlight would be dim, similar to a light beam traveling through polluted water.

EYE SPY

Like fingerprints, our irises are unique. Just as we use fingerprints to help identify people, an optical sensor called an eye scanner can identify people by their irises. But things can get in the way—like eyelashes or glasses. Some scientists have come up with a solution by designing a scanner that would sense whole faces as well as irises. The scanner takes a video image of the face and iris. Then it checks a database. If the person is in the database, he or she can be identified by the scanner. This type of identification could become a common security measure in the future.

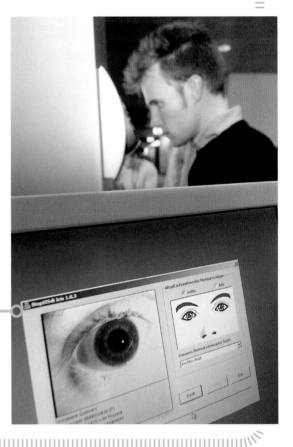

Some airports around the world already use eye scanners at security checkpoints.

A water treatment engineer uses a sensor to test the water quality.

The more pollution, the more the light is reduced. At the other end of the sensor, the detector senses the beam of light. The detector measures how much light is received at a specific wavelength and converts this measurement into an electronic signal. Scientists use the information in this signal to figure out how polluted the water is.

CHAPTER FOUR

TOUCH, SMELL, AND TASTE

The senses of sound and sight help us find objects, communicate, and avoid potential danger. Our senses of touch, smell, and taste might seem less important, but they can help us avoid danger too. They also make our lives much more fun. Think what it would be like if you couldn't smell fresh-baked cookies. The human senses of touch, smell, and taste can all be replicated by artificial sensors.

TOUCH

We have sensors all over our skin. Millions of nerve endings in your skin can detect stimuli such as hot or cold temperatures. They can also detect pressure. When we touch something, these sensors send a signal to the brain. This signal goes through the nervous system the same way signals do for sight and sound. Signals from your skin go to the part of the brain that interprets touch, pain, and pressure. It happens very quickly. Your brain can identify a hot object and send a signal to pull back from it before you get burned.

Touch sensors on devices like robotic vacuums are called tactile sensors. Tactile sensors are sensitive to touch or pressure. Your

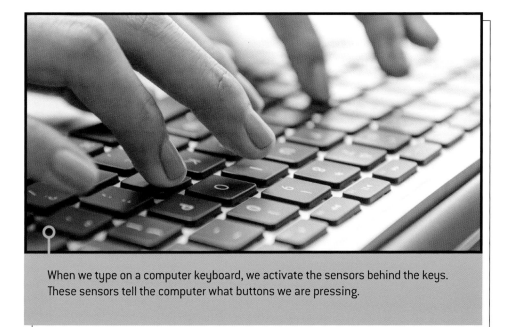

When we type on a computer keyboard, we activate the sensors behind the keys. These sensors tell the computer what buttons we are pressing.

parents might have a touch sensor on a key chain that unlocks a car. The sensor senses when a button on the key chain is pressed and sends a signal to the car's computer, telling it to unlock the door. Touch screens on tablets and similar devices also have tactile sensors. A computer keyboard has touch sensors too. They tell the computer what keys are being pressed. We use touch sensors on many appliances and devices.

To understand how touch sensors work, let's think about a simple example. A doorbell is a tactile sensor. The stimulus is your finger, which is pressing the doorbell. When the doorbell is pressed, it creates a closed path that allows electricity to flow, known as a circuit. Doorbell buttons can be simple switches, meaning they close a circuit. This sends a small amount of power to ring the bell.

DIAGRAM OF A DOORBELL

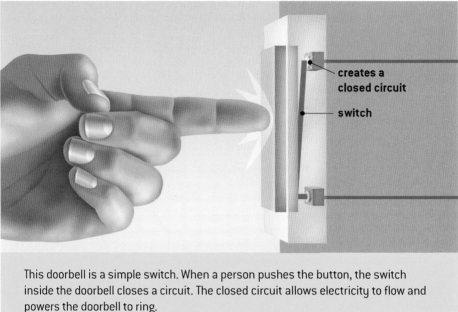

creates a
closed circuit

switch

This doorbell is a simple switch. When a person pushes the button, the switch inside the doorbell closes a circuit. The closed circuit allows electricity to flow and powers the doorbell to ring.

Doorbell buttons can also have an electromagnet, a coil of wire wrapped around metal. When the electricity flows, it passes through the wire and makes a magnetic field. The magnetic field powers the mechanism that creates the response. The response is a bell, buzzer, or chime. In some doorbells, the mechanism is a magnetic piece that strikes two tone bars. These two bars make the *ding-dong* sound.

SMELL

Remember the last time you took out the garbage? You might have wished for a weaker sense of smell. Our sense of smell works when we breathe in small molecules. These molecules are in the air all

A DOG'S NOSE KNOWS

With about three hundred million smell receptors in their noses, dogs can identify many more smells than humans, who have only six million. Dogs can smell ten thousand to one hundred thousand times better than people.

Dogs might be good models for scientists who want to build smelling robots. Building a robot with a sense of smell is harder than building one that can see or hear because smelling is very complex. Light and sound signals are conveyed through specific types of energy, but to have the ability to smell, one must detect thousands of different particles in the air. A robot bloodhound is probably a long way off.

around us. After you breathe them in, they contact nerve endings inside your nose. The nerve endings translate the molecules into electrical signals and send them through the nervous system to your brain. Your brain identifies the smell. It might send you a signal to plug your nose. You might even gag.

Some sensors detect gases and chemicals similar to the way the nose smells. Carbon monoxide (CO) detectors detect a gas that can be harmful to people. People can't smell or see CO, so these detectors let people know when too much CO is in the air.

When carbon monoxide fills a carbon monoxide detector, sensors detect a chemical reaction. This causes the detector to sound an alarm.

One type of CO detector has sensors inside a case with tiny holes in it. These sensors contain a working electrode—the part of a sensor where an electric current enters or leaves. When CO is in the air, it flows through the holes in the case and reaches the working electrode. This starts a chemical reaction where the CO combines with oxygen and changes to carbon dioxide. This causes ions, tiny molecules with an electrical charge, to flow through to a second electrode called the counter electrode. The two electrodes are then connected in a circuit. The electric current that flows between the two electrodes measures the amount of CO in the air. If the level is too high, an alarm sounds.

TASTE

Think about taking a bite of cheesy pizza or a juicy orange. Taste gives humans pleasure. Taste helps us test the food we eat, since we could get sick or die from eating the wrong food. A bitter taste might mean poisonous food. A sour taste might mean rotting food.

Human taste sensors are hard to replicate. After all, we can taste about one hundred thousand different flavors. Scientists have designed an electronic tongue, a handheld device that food

When you drink a glass of pink lemonade, the taste sensors on your tongue react to both the sour and sweet flavors in the drink.

companies can use instead of human taste testers. The device works by transforming different tastes to electric signals. These electric signals are entered into a computer. The computer takes the place of the human brain and registers a taste, like sweet or salty. These artificial tongues test for the quality of coffee, water, and other drinks. They can sense germs in water. They can also sense small amounts of sugar and salt that humans can't detect.

SOLVE IT!

SENSORS IN THE STORE

Think back to the introduction. Remember all the events that happened during your trip to the store? Which types of sensors were used for each event or device? *(The answer key is on page 35.)*

CHAPTER FIVE

SUPER SENSES

Many sensors are based on human senses, but some sensors can do even more. They see, hear, or feel *better* than people. Some sensors can detect things that humans can't. Scientists have also designed some completely new senses, like radar.

Radar stands for radio detecting and ranging. During World War I (1914–1918), airplanes were a big threat. Planes were fast, so it was hard for soldiers on the ground to shoot them down without advance warning. But scientists were working on a way to sense faraway planes. By World War II (1939–1945), planes were detected with devices that used radio waves. These sensors could detect planes that were up to 100 miles (160 kilometers) away.

Radar has a transmitter that sends out a pulse of radio waves. A receiver

This radar display shows two warplanes detected in the distance.

then looks for radio waves that get reflected back. The time taken for the wave to return is used to detect distance.

Modern drones are also called UAVs, or unmanned aerial vehicles. Drones use many sensors to help them work. Drones can collect data from inside volcanoes using optical sensors, and they can use tactile sensors to reach out and collect a rock sample. Drones with optical sensors can also survey forest fires. Rescue drones use optical sensors to help find crash victims.

A drone flies around an active volcano to research a crater made from a volcanic eruption. This helps scientists learn about volcanoes when they are too dangerous to approach.

Matthew Newbury was the first person in the United Kingdom to be fitted with a bionic prosthetic leg.

Farmers can use drones with infrared sensors to monitor the health of crops. Healthy plants have lots of chlorophyll, a pigment that reflects infrared light. So having these sensors inside a drone is a great tool. Farmers can sense whether crops need water.

Bionics are artificial body parts. For these body parts to work, they need sensors. Bionic body parts process and turn sensor data into signals they send to the brain. The goal of bionic research is to restore body parts. These body parts may have been lost in an accident. Bionic limbs use tactile sensors to sense their surroundings. New bionic legs can sense the angle of a metal foot as it swings forward. Scientists have also made bionic eyes with optical sensors to help blind people.

Radar, drones, and bionics were all designed by scientists and

Darwin

Darwin is a wheeled robot made by scientists to learn how the brain works. He has ninety thousand virtual neurons, or nerve cells. *Virtual* means that the nerve cells don't really exist as they do in humans. They're modeled with software on Darwin's computer. Darwin's virtual brain is about the size of a snail's. He's helping scientists learn how information from sensors is interpreted by computers and how the brain learns to navigate.

engineers to improve on what humans can accomplish. Just as our five senses help us, high-tech sensors do too. They help us monitor the environment, keep us safe, and make life easier.

REMOTE REFLECTION

See for yourself how a sensor works! In this science project, you'll test whether you can turn on your TV without pointing the remote directly at the screen using different household objects. Most of these supplies should be easy to find at home, but ask an adult if you need help finding them or getting set up.

WHAT YOU'LL NEED

- a writing utensil
- a piece of paper
- a TV and its remote
- a small mirror
- a sheet of aluminum foil
- a book

WHAT YOU'LL DO

1. Make a two-column table to record your findings. The first column will list which item you're testing (the mirror, aluminum foil, or book). In the next few columns, write down whether or not the TV was able to turn on, how close you were standing to the TV, and any other observations you have.
2. With the TV off, turn your back to the TV and look in the mirror so that you can see the TV behind you.
3. Point the remote into the mirror at the TV and press the On button. Did it work?
4. If not, try moving a little closer to the TV or adjusting the mirror.
5. Try using the aluminum foil. With your back to the TV, point the remote toward the foil and press the On button.
6. This time, try the experiment with a book. You can keep it closed or open to a random page. Keep your back to the TV, point the remote at the book, and press the On button.

FOLLOW-UP

Which item or items worked to turn on the TV? Which didn't? Why do you think certain items did and some didn't? What are the similarities and differences among the item or items that worked compared to the item or items that didn't?

THE POWER OF LIGHTS (PAGE 21)

The light sensor in your TV is designed to only pick up on infrared light waves, such as those sent by your TV remote. The other lights in a room have visible light waves, so the TV's sensor wouldn't react to them.

SENSORS IN THE STORE (PAGE 29)

In order: the doors opened with an optical sensor, the restroom lights turned on with a motion sensor, the checkout clerk used an optical sensor to scan items and their price, and the credit card scanner read the card's information with an optical sensor.

GLOSSARY

amplitude: the measurement of the height of a wave

coordinator: the part of a device that interprets a signal and sends a command to the effector

data: information that can be transmitted in the form of electrical signals

effector: the part of a device that causes a response

electric current: the flow of electricity

electrode: the part of a sensor where an electric current enters or leaves

frequency: the number of times something happens in a given time period

hertz: the unit used to measure frequency. One hertz is equal to one wave cycle per second.

interpret: to explain the meaning of something

molecule: a group of atoms bonded together

optical sensor: a sensor that detects light waves

pigment: a natural coloring substance in plants and animals

radio wave: an electromagnetic wave often used for communication

response: a reaction to something

signal: a sound, motion, or other form of information that a sensor can detect

stimulus: any type of input signal. A stimulus causes a response. The plural form of *stimulus* is *stimuli*.

tactile sensor: also known as a touch sensor, a sensor that is sensitive to touch or pressure

wave: a traveling disturbance that moves through space and matter, moving energy from one place to another

SELECTED BIBLIOGRAPHY

Beiser, Arthur. *Physics.* 5th ed. Reading, MA: Addison-Wesley, 1992.

Brain, Marshall. *The Engineering Book: From the Catapult to the Curiosity Rover; 250 Milestones in the History of Engineering.* New York: Sterling, 2015.

"Electricity and Sensors." University of Waikato, September 2, 2010. http://sciencelearn.org.nz/Contexts/Super-Sense/Science-Ideas-and-Concepts/Electricity-and-sensors.

McGrath, Michael J., and Cliodhna N. Scanaill. *Sensor Technologies: Healthcare, Wellness and Environmental Applications.* New York: ApressOpen, 2014.

Wilson, Daniel H. *Robots: A New Age of Bionics, Drones and Artificial Intelligence.* New York: Hearst Books, 2015.

LERNER

SOURCE™

Expand learning beyond the printed book. Download free, complementary educational resources for this book from our website, www.lerneresource.com.

Ceceri, Kathy. *Robotics: Discover the Science and Technology of the Future with 20 Projects.* White River Junction, VT: Nomad, 2012.
Read more about designing robots and even build your own using craft materials and recycled household items.

Deane-Pratt, Ade. *Sensors.* New York: PowerKids, 2012.
See many examples of sensors with scientific explanations of how they work.

Murphy, Maggie. *High-Tech DIY Projects with Electronics, Sensors, and LEDs.* New York: PowerKids, 2015.
Learn more about building your own sensors and electronic devices.

Robotics: Facts
http://idahoptv.org/sciencetrek/topics/robots/facts.cfm
Learn more information on robotics, like different ways they use sensors, and find links to games.

Rowell, Rebecca. *Energy and Waves through Infographics.* Minneapolis: Lerner Publications, 2014.
Look at charts, illustrations, and maps to learn more about how sound and energy travel.

Science with Kids
http://sciencewithkids.com/science-facts/infrared-ir-sensor.html
This site explains the history of infrared light and some uses for infrared sensors in our homes.

Wavelength
http://www.windows2universe.org/physical_science/basic_tools/wavelength.html
Check out this site for more information about waves and wavelength.

INDEX

PHOTO ACKNOWLEDGMENTS